The Pathway of Life

by Beryl Wicker

Published by
Filament Publishing Ltd
16, Croydon Road, Beddington,
Croydon, Surrey CR0 4PA

+44(0) 20 8688 2598
www.filamentpublishing.com

© 2021 Beryl Wicker
ISBN 978-1-913623-71-5

The right to be recognised as the author of this work has been asserted by Beryl Wicker in accordance with the Designs and copyrights Act 1988 Section 77.

All Rights Reserved
No portion of this work may be copied without the prior written permission of the publisher

Printed in the UK by 4Edge

What people are saying....

These comments were made about Beryl's second book, The Patchwork of Life:

Your poems are delightful, being easily read and giving pictures of daily living, but they often deal with the major issues of life. I sat and read them all, and now I must re-read them; they are so full of lovely images.

John and Shirley Richer

Your book of poems is excellent, so readable and enjoyable. I took it to bed with me one night and read almost to the end! So well-produced with very suitable illustrations. Altogether a wonderful book to follow its predecessor!

Rev. Adrian Smith

I love poetry and your poems are so evocative of former and the present-day bringing feelings of nostalgia and also of the reality of this last year. Most of all they are enjoyable to read with their humour and poignancy. Through all your wisdom, faith shines through and so 'The Patchwork of Life' is a real blessing.

Andrew and Fiona Fleet

Thank you for my Christmas presents, but my favourite item was your second book of poetry. I read it cover to cover on Christmas Day.

Jane – Beryl's grand daughter

We are writing to let you know how much we have enjoyed reading your latest collection of poems 'The Patchwork of Life'. You have a special gift which you share with so many people. You are able to incorporate everyday life in your poems, whether situations have been sad and emotional or light hearted and funny. Anyone who has been fortunate to read either one or both of your books, will certainly have had their spirits lifted during these very difficult times.

Cheryl and Ian Hirst

I'm reading your book little by little with a dictionary in my hand. It's very interesting. I'm enjoying it.

Yoko Hasegawa – a Japanese friend living in Tokyo

Your poems are amazing! I was going to read one a night before bed, but I read at least eight last night! Your gift for writing is extraordinary and I am so glad you are sharing them.

Megan (Faringdon)

I loved reading your poems. Some make me nostalgic for the days of my youth, others make me smile, but the poem content always brings a tear.

Mary (London)

The Author

Beryl Wicker was born in 1928 in Swindon to May and Sydney Gee. Her father was a blacksmith and a local Methodist Preacher.

Beryl has been an active member of the Highworth Methodist Church for much of her life, organising many fund-raising events. This year, 2021, at the age of 93, she is busy organising the Church Christmas Bazaar!

On leaving school, Beryl trained as a nurse at the Royal National Orthopaedic Hospital and the West London General Hospital. She met her husband, Alan, in London and they married in 1950. After their daughters, Susan and Mirian were born, Beryl left nursing and studied Poetry and Drama, winning the gold medal from the London Academy of Music and Dramatic Art. She taught this subject for many years and has had several of her poems published.

Beryl and Alan moved to Highworth, Wiltshire in 1979 and they have six grandchildren and six great grandchildren. Beryl has previously had two books of her poems published. The first was The Tapestry of Life in 2019, the second was

The Patchwork of Life in 2020. This, The Pathway of Life will be the third.

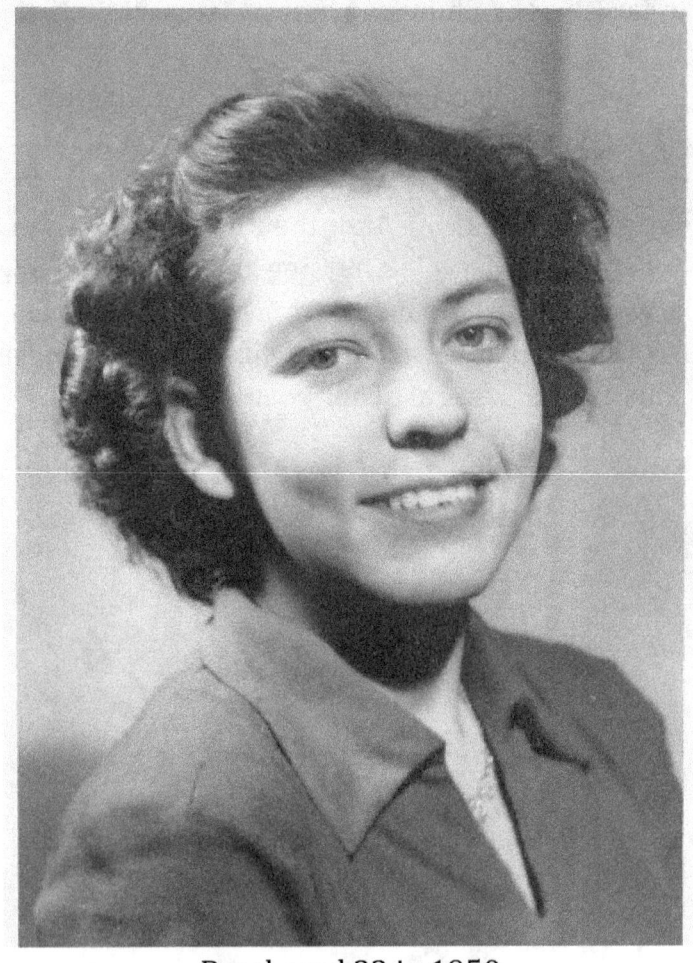

Beryl aged 22 in 1950

Acknowledgements

I would like to thank everyone who has supported me by purchasing, reading and recommending my poetry books, The Tapestry of Life and The Patchwork of Life. The wonderful messages I have received have been very encouraging.

Thank you once again to my publisher, Chris Day and his team at Filament Publishing for all their help and excellent production.

Thank you to my family and friends for all their help and encouragement, especially my daughter, Mirian, for providing the photographs of pathways found in this book, which were taken on her walks. Also, many thanks to Mirian, and Peter McAuley for proof reading this book.

Once again, I must thank my friend, Val McAuley for all she has done to make my poetry books possible. She has encouraged and supported me and spent hours turning my handwritten poems into beautiful books.

Beryl and Alan's Wedding in 1950

Contents

Foreword	11
The Pathway of Life	13
Meditation	14
The Gift	15
Spring	16
Reflections	17
The Squatters	18
Heaven Sent	19
Fear Not	20
A Peaceful Day	21
Morning Glory	23
A Good Decision	24
From my Garden	25
On the Bus	26
Covid Pandemic	28
Frustration 2021 – Covid Virus	30
Bubble Trouble	33
Be Careful What You Wish For	34
Little Things	36
Rejoice	38
Cup Final: England versus Italy 2021	40
The Future	43
A Vision	44
A Visit to The New Room, Bristol, John Wesley's Chapel	45
Wesley's Wise Words	47
If Only…	49
A Sorry Tale	50
Lonely	52

Devotion	53
Beauty and Heartache	55
Alone	56
After Sunday Worship	57
White Horse Hill	58
Memories	59
Simpler Times	61
Childhood Memories	62
Today and Yester Year	64
Please Mum	66
Why?	68
Good Morning, Bill	69
Trevor	71
Bill and Trevor	72
Holy Howlers	74
Have You Ever Seen an Angel?	76
Nobody	78
Destination	79
Mrs Brown	81
That Naughty Imp	83
I Wish	85
The Bright Side	87
I Don't Understand	88
The Prodigal Son	90
Seeking the Lost	93
The Good Samaritan	96
Hand in Hand	99
A Rough Patch	101
Life's Pathway	103

Foreword

This is Beryl's third book of poetry, written throughout the Covid pandemic 2020-21 while in her nineties. I never cease to be amazed at Beryl's ability to continue to write so many poems. She says it 'keeps her brain active' and has kept her going through the lockdowns due to the pandemic.

Her positive attitude to life is inspiring. She sees the funny side of situations and is always enthralled with the beauty of God's creation. These qualities are expressed so beautifully in her poetry, which has been a blessing to so many people.

Beryl has a strong Christian faith and this Bible verse from Psalm 73:26 perhaps explains who she gets her strength from:

'My flesh and my heart may fail, but God is the strength of my heart and my portion for ever.'

Val McAuley
Highworth, Wiltshire 2021

The Pathway of Life

Let me walk with you, on this pathway,
On this pathway of life.
I'll be by your side when the going gets tough
And carry you through, when the pathway is rough.
When the path is steep and the way is narrow
I'll walk ahead so that you can follow.
Just keep your eyes on me.

When the path is smooth and the way ahead clear,
And the songs of the birds fill the trees,
And the kiss of the sun opens the flowers
For the butterflies and bees;
When the sun shines brightly in the azure sky,
And soft breezes stroke the warm weather,
Let us sing with pure joy as we walk on life's path
And give thanks that we walk it together.

Meditation

Inspired by a yellow pansy in my garden path

Dear Pansy, with your velvet smile;
I hope you'll stay with me a while.
You weren't here yesterday, I know,
But now you've pushed up through the snow.

The ground below is cold and hard;
No soil is there, it's just a yard
Where such frail strength, where such sweet beauty?
'God gave me power to do my duty'.

When the pathway through life is bereft of all light
And we lose the will to go on,
Let us think of the pansy bursting through the dark ground
And shedding its beauty around.

He lay in the darkness in a borrowed tomb.
He'd walked the pathway of pain.
In the fullness of time, He burst forth from the ground
And shed His glory around.

The Gift

This poem came to me as I looked from my window on a windy winter's day.

Have you seen the snowflakes on a windy day?
They dance and they prance as they make their way
To the frozen ground below.

Have you seen the little birds,
Looking for crumbs in the snow?
And have you heard the crack of the ice,
As the daffodils push from the darkness below?

Have you smelt the musk of the fox,
As it hunts a meal for its cubs?
Have you felt the warmth of the sun
And seen the trees springing buds?

This is the world that God has made
As a gift for all mankind,
To be treasured and nurtured and treated with care:
A world that our children are happy to share,
A world that is just as God planned.
Let us care for our beautiful land.

Spring

Spring has sprung in my garden;
Green shoots have pushed through the ground,
Myriad birds in the sycamore tree
Are making a glorious sound.

I sit at my open window and watch the world go by;
Children on their way to school, the postman on his bike,
The old chap with his newspaper
And the toddler on his trike.

My mind goes back to long ago
When we children played in the street
With the skipping rope stretched across the road
And swung beneath our feet.

Then the pitter, pitter pat of the soft spring rain
Draws me back to the present again.
The birds sing louder and the snowdrops glisten,
A snail slides over the lawn,
The air is filled with the scent of the soil
As spring is being reborn.

Reflections

The sun is a great big red balloon.
On this April morning, it floods my room
With its harsh bright light, no corner is spared
From its probing fingers and mighty glare.

Last night, my room was silvery bright,
When a saucer of moon filled the corners with light.
Each globe has its place in the vastness of space,
God gave them power and authority.

The earth spins round and the tides ebb and flow;
The faithful flowers, in my garden, grow.
The insects creep for cover when the morning birds arrive.
Bees seek out the pollen and take it to their hive.

Storm clouds gather and the world is washed clean.
Then, a light wind blows and the sun beams on high;
He bends the bow on the knee of heaven
And places it in the sky.

The Squatters
This is an annual event.

The summer, my friend, is just round the corner.
The trees are springing new leaves,
Wild daffodils blow in the hedgerows below
And starlings nest in the eaves.

I hear them shuffling in the roof, overhead,
As I lay down, to sleep, each night in my bed.
And then, some weeks later, chirping and cheeping
Enters my dreams while I am sleeping.

The babies are hatching and need to be fed
With fat juicy worms and small crumbs of bread.
I hope when my lodgers are ready to fly,
I'll be there to see them take to the sky.

Heaven Sent

Dawn chorus day, May 2nd 2021

A blackbird was practicing his flute, all day
And on a roof, not far away, a chorus of birds sang
a round a lay.

A sparrow and a starling, a robin and a wren,
A blackbird and a thrush sang again and again.
A tap, tap, tap was heard on the trunk of a tree;
A woodpecker bird tapped out a melody.

So, then, they all kept time, the sound they made, divine.
They sang until the moon rose in the sky.
Then, they folded up their wings and dreamed
of secret things,
Till a light breeze stroked the morning sky.

The woodpecker tapped his beak, the birds
aroused from sleep;
The promise of a fine day lay before us;
The blackbird played the note
And from each feathery throat
Arose a glorious dawn chorus.

Fear Not

FOR I KNOW THE PLANS I HAVE FOR YOU,
" DECLARES THE LORD, "PLANS TO PROSPER YOU
AND NOT TO HARM YOU, PLANS
TO GIVE YOU HOPE AND A FUTURE.
JEREMIAH 29:11

The ditches glow with the promise of summer;
Celandines, golden, reflect the sun's rays.
Dainty forget-me-nots spread a blue carpet,
A blackbird pipes a hymn of praise.

A virus lays its vicious carpet
And seeks to smother all mankind.
It creeps along life's pathways
And infiltrates the mind.

But it can't destroy the promise of summer.
It can't destroy God's plan.
The flowers will bloom and the birds will sing
And the virus will bow at the feet of the King

A Peaceful Day

*When I was a child, I used to love to cycle in
the Wiltshire countryside.*

It's a glorious day today, not a cloud in the sky.
The only sound is the hum of the bees
And the gentle rustle of the leaves on the trees.
Then, a butterfly lands on my bike.

I raise my eyes to the distant hills
Etched out against the sky,
And then, to the valley in the deepening shadows,
Where I know a river flows by.

The butterfly spreads its ivory wings
And lifts itself in flight.
Such a delicate creature, I pray for its safety,
As it flutters out of my sight.

I sit me down in the meadow flowers
And watch the grazing sheep.
The gentle breeze from the sycamore trees
Lulls me into sleep.

I dream of the distant hills and I dream of the valley below.
I dream of the butterfly, spreading its wings
And deciding which way to go.
I dream of the meadow flowers and I dream
of the shady tree.
Then, I hear the voice of my mother,
Calling me home to tea.

Morning Glory

I drew back the curtains and the world was golden.
The leafless trees were tinged with pink
Unseen birds sang their special songs,
As the sun crept, silently, over the brink.

Had I not woken at six that morning
And drawn back the curtains, to let in the light,
I would have missed that magical moment
When day triumphed over the darkness of night.

A Good Decision

The north wind shrieks across the hill,
The storm clouds gather and the wind is chill.
The lightning flashes and the thunder roars;
I'm not going out – I'll stay indoors.

From My Garden

God looked at his creation and saw that it was good.

Come, stroll with me in my garden,
In this hour twixt day and night,
When the sun slips away to a foreign land
And the moon floods my garden with light.

Breathe in the scent of the roses,
As it floats on the evening breeze.
Hear the cheep of the weary birds,
As they settle among the trees.

Raise your eyes to the heavens;
Ponder the vastness of space.
See the planets and stars that came into existence,
When God uncovered his face.

On the Bus

This poem has several difficult rhythms.
It's better to read it aloud. Don't forget to use
separate voices for A and B.

A: Hello, Ada, come and sit by me;
Have you been shopping today?

B: I've bought a nice bit of haddock
For my husband's tea. He likes a bit of fish on a Friday.

A: Do you know that Lil, who lives over the hill?
Well, she's dyed her hair bright green.

B: Do you mean that woman who is married to a Fred,
Who drives round in a lorry?
They've got a son who's married
To a girl called Florrie?

A: Do you mean that Florrie, who worked in the café
Over in market street?
She dropped a hot teapot on the café floor
And scalded a customer's feet.

A: Florrie was in trouble and the woman was in shock.
They took her to the A&E
Her husband sued the shop and Florrie got the chop,
But nobody paid for the tea.

B: I think I saw that lady, in town, the other day;
She had slippers on her feet and was walking with a stick.
Her husband was beside her
And I think she called him Vic.

A: Is that the Vic, who has a son,
Married to a Trish?
Oh, I think this is your bus stop;
Don't forget your fish!

Covid Pandemic

Be prepared for the various rhythms in this poem. It's better to read it aloud.

Softly, silently, while we slept,
The killer virus stealthily crept.
When the world awoke the following morning,
Life was changed, without any warning.

Wash your hands,
Stay indoors,
Wear a mask,
Obey the laws,
Work at home if you are able,
Teach the children at the kitchen table.

The world is enmeshed in a web of death.
The government gets the blame!
Scientists are working day and night;
'We'll find a vaccine', they claim.

Doctors and nurses are working long hours,
Fighting an unknown disease,
While hundreds of thousands of people are dying,
Losing their power to breathe.

A form of madness hits the shops.
A fight breaks out in the aisle,

As two men fight over toilet rolls.
The manager hides a smile.

We grieve that our loved ones are dying without us;
A nurse holds on to their hand.
We wait by the phone to be told of their passing
And know that they dwell in a better land.

Days are getting shorter and nights are getting darker.
Young families find life's a struggle.
Residents in care homes feel they've been forgotten.
All they want is family to cuddle.

The pathway through life is getting rough;
The way ahead is steep.
Some folk fall by the wayside
And some sit down and weep.

I see a glimmer of life ahead.
I feel anticipation.
A sign post at the crossroads states:
THIS WAY FOR THE VACCINATION.

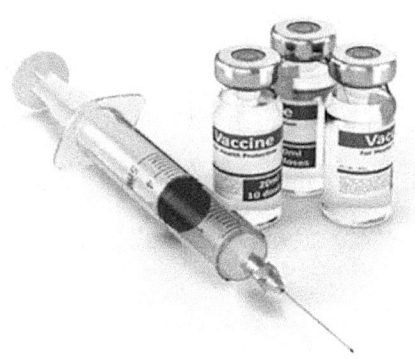

Frustration 2021 – Covid Virus

I think I'll go shopping, there are things I must get;
I'll not write a list, I never forget.
I put on my coat, my gloves and my scarf,
My hearing aid, glasses, my stick and my mask.

I get to the shop, wipe my hands with some gel.
Then, my glasses steam up and I can't see too well!
I take off my glasses, hold them in my hand
And walk down the aisle to buy what I've planned.

What's in that punnet, just out of my reach?
I can't read the label, is it plums, is it peach?
I look for some milk; it's on the top shelf.
I stand on my tiptoes, but can't help myself!

My stick falls off from my arm, to the floor;
A man picks it up, oh good, he is tall,
'Can you, please, reach some milk? I don't like to ask.'
'No problem', he says. 'Thanks', I smile, in my mask.

Then, to the next aisle, for some bread and some cake.
My glasses steam up, so I can't read the date!
So, off come my glasses – my hearing aid, too.
I'm fed up with shopping, I know what I'll do.

I pay for my milk and hurry back home.
Take off my mask and pick up the phone,
'Good morning', I say, 'Put me out of my misery
And book for me – a HOME DELIVERY!'

Bubble Trouble

Boris said we should form a bubble
And meet our friends outdoors.
So, we carried the table into the garden
To follow old Boris's laws.

We sat round the table, six feet apart,
While father carved the meat.
Then a strong wind blew up and tugged at the cloth
And the gravy spilled over our feet!

Our dinner grew cold and as rain sheeted down;
Soaking wet, we ran in for cover.
We stood there, dripping, six feet apart.
'It's Boris' fault', says my brother.

Mother, upset, said she'd never forget
How she'd gone to so much trouble.
Then, Dad, with a grin, fetched a large pin
And said 'I'll burst his bubble!'

Be Careful What You Wish For (May 2021)

We're coming out of lockdown.
The children are back at their schools.
We can see all our friends again,
As long as we follow the rules.

I go to the café for coffee
To drink outside, in the cold.
Then, along to the book shop, to buy some cards;
Two allowed in, at a time, I am told.

I wait outside; it starts to rain.
The path gets flooded; there are leaves in the drain.
I go down the street, for a haircut.
When I get there, it is shut!

I'm freezing cold and soaking wet.
This life is not for me.
I'd rather be in lockdown;
I think you must agree.

I paddle back the way I came,
So glad to be at home.
Then, warm and dry, I settle down
Beside my friend – the 'phone!

Little Things

It's the little things in life that make a difference,
The little things that make the world go round,
It's the little things we do and the little things we say
That effect those whom we meet on life's journey,
day by day.

A little pinch of salt will add flavour to the greens,
And a little bit of help will string the runner beans,
A little tiny baby, and a little bit of sleep,
A little bit of money to see us through the week.

A little bit of chocolate and a little bit of rest,
A little grateful smile when your husband does his best,
A little card of thanks when someone does a favour,
And a little kindly visit to a lonely neighbour.

But the things that bother me, I think you will agree,
Are the little things that we can't see.
They give us coughs and colds and 'flu
And gastro-enteritis too!
Yes ....
It's the little things in life that make a difference!

Rejoice

Rejoice with me, brothers and sisters,
The church is open today.
So, put on your masks and your hand gel,
Bow your heads and pray.

Rejoice with me, little children,
You can go out and play.
Get out your bike and your roller skates
And enjoy yourselves today.

Rejoice with me, all you teachers,
Zoom is a thing of the past.
The children are back in school today,
So, you can teach them in class.

Rejoice with me, you workers,
Do you still want to work from home?
You have a choice, so use your voice
And speak to your boss, on the phone.

We rejoice with the scientists.
We rejoice with the hospital staff.
We'll never forget their dedication,
As they've led us along life's path.

The National health has a birthday.
Today it is seventy-three.
The Queen has awarded it the George Cross
On behalf of you and me.

Let us rejoice in the present.
Let the past take care of the past.
Leave the future in the hands of God,
As we continue along life's path.

Cup Final: England versus Italy 2021

This is the last of 100 poems written during Lock-down.

I'm not a lover of football,
But I'm quite patriotic;
So, when England was in the Final,
I thought I'd sit down and watch it.

There were twenty men chasing a ball, a man in a net at each end.
I expect they wanted to join in and play.
They danced and they pranced, but when they got their chance
They kicked the football away!

There were thousands of people watching the game.
They booed or cheered all the night.
Some of the men took off their tops,
Which wasn't a pretty sight!

When a man in white kicked the ball in the net,
The rest of his team knocked him down!
The crowd shouted and cheered and threw up their hats,
As the poor man lay on the ground.

A whistle blew, for them to rest.
They went into a huddle,
A man, in a suit talked to them
And gave each one a cuddle!

The game started again and two men collided.
They hit the ground quite hard.
A man in pink ran over the field
And showed them a yellow card.

That was a very strange thing to do.
Why didn't he wait 'til the end?
That wasn't the time or the place for a chat,
There's a football match to attend.

Ten minutes later, the game stopped again;
A man on the ground was writhing in pain.
A doctor ran on, black bag in hand.
He examined the man and helped him to stand.

He hopped off the field and another ran on.
The crowd loudly cheered and broke forth into song.
I was feeling quite sleepy and frankly, was bored,
So, I closed my eyes and the other side scored!

The game continued; the men chased the ball;
The ones in their nets were rehearsing their steps.
They lunged and they skipped and they kicked at the ball,
Which flew down the field, so no goal was scored.

They played extra time; will this game never end?
Who invented the ball? Do tell me, my friend?
A mighty roar erupts from the crowd; the game
is over and done.
I think it's a shame, at the end of the game, that neither
side has won.

But, before I could turn off the set, ten men stood in front of
the net.
They took it in turns to kick the ball.
The goal keepers started to dance once more.
The huge crowd held its breath, what happened
next was such a pity.
England lost...... the winner was Italy.

The Future

This poem popped into my head before I got up this morning.

A silence, profound, filled my bedroom,
Which was lit by an eerie light.
I drew back the curtains and looked from my window;
The world had transformed overnight.

All colour had gone from my garden,
The pavements had gone from the street,
The earth had been wrapped in a blanket of snow
And laid, pristine at my feet.

A strong wind gathered the clouds from the sky,
Scattered snow on the face of the moon.
Then, I knew what was meant by climate change,
Because it was only June.

A Vision

I dream of a world that is soft and green;
A world where flowers never die.
I dream of a world where the streams run clean;
Where fish swim safely by.

I dream of a land where the trees grow tall
And nourish the earth with its rain.
I dream of a time when the sun shines bright
And ripens the golden grain.

I dream of a world where the lion and lamb,
Together, lie down in the den,
And a small child makes friends with a poisonous snake
And the hawk will nest with the wren.

I long for a land where disease is no more,
And hunger and warfare will cease.
Where all mankind will care for each other
And everyone live in peace.
Amen

A Visit to The New Room, Bristol, John Wesley's Chapel

Beryl and Phyllis Rogers - March 2019

Having fun dressing up with Val and Phyllis in
The New Room

Wesley's Wise Words

The Methodist Church was founded by John Wesley who was born in 1703. I thought these items make interesting reading:

John Wesley's Manifesto

1. Reduce the gap between rich people and poor people
2. Help everyone to have a job
3. Help the poorest, including introducing a living wage
4. Offer the best possible education
5. Help everyone to feel they can make a difference
6. Promote tolerance
7. Promote equal treatment for women
8. Create a society based on values and not on profits and consumerism
9. End all forms of slavery
10. Avoid getting into wars
11. Share the love of God with everyone
12. Care for the environment

DO ALL THE GOOD YOU CAN,
BY ALL THE MEANS YOU CAN,
IN ALL THE WAYS YOU CAN,
IN ALL THE PLACES YOU CAN,
AT ALL THE TIMES YOU CAN,
TO ALL THE PEOPLE YOU CAN,
AS LONG AS EVER YOU CAN.

- JOHN WESLEY -

Wesley And Well-Being

John Wesley was way ahead of his time in promoting the value of prevention rather than cure.

He recommended:

KEEPING CLEAN

'Every one that would preserve health should be as clean and sweet as possible in their houses, clothes and furniture... Cleanliness is next to Godliness.'

DRINKING WATER

'Water is the wholesomest of all drinks; it quickens the appetite and strengthens the digestion most.'

EATING PLAIN FOOD

'Abstain from all pickled, smoked or high-seasoned food... Use a plain diet, easy of digestion and eat such quantity of food as sits light upon the stomach.'

REGULAR EXERCISE

'Exercise is of greater service to your health than a hundred medicines.'

The things to avoid were:

EXCESS SALT

'Salted food is unwholesome.'

ALCOHOLIC SPIRITS

'Spirituous liquors are a certain, though slow, poison.'

SITTING DOWN TOO MUCH

'Those who read or write much should learn to do it standing.'

BECOMING OVERWEIGHT

He suggested a weight loss regime that was similar to the modern 'Cabbage Soup Diet'

Wesley also advised against smoking tobacco, not because he knew of its impact on the lungs, but because it destroyed people's teeth.

The most important thing of all to maintain your health was to have **'PEACE OF MIND'** because '... **the passions have a greater influence upon health than most people are aware of.'**

Wesley thought faith was the best solution to achieving peace of mind:

'The love of God... as it is the sovereign remedy of all miseries... by the unspeakable joy and perfect calm, serenity, and tranquility it gives the mind, becomes the most powerful... of all the means of health and long life.'

If Only....

Love grew wings and flew to the earth,
Intending to spread itself around.
But when it saw the state of the world,
It knew it needed a friend.

So, it sent for understanding,
To come and play its part.
With eyes full of love, it looked at mankind
And sprinkled itself in each heart.

Then, peace came down to join them
And together, they stood, hand in hand.
Heaven's arches rang, as the angels sang
And God's glory flooded the land.

A Sorry Tale

Not what was intended!

A rickety bridge spans the river,
Where the children hang upside down
And lovers stroll in the fading twilight
After the sun sinks down.

A swan, on its nest, sits protecting its eggs;
Coots on the water, do sleep
And the rickety bridge keeps an eye on them all.
They say still waters run deep!

When the bridge was erected in 1709,
It was sturdy and firm and strong,
But the sands of time have taken their toll
And they say the bridge won't last long.

'That never will do', say the lovers.
'Please help it', the children implore.
So, the men of the village come down with their tools,
Fresh wood, a hammer and saw.

The rickety bridge holds its breath;

The swans look on in awe,

As the villagers set to work, with a will.

Now, the rickety bridge

Is ……

No more!

Lonely

The old man stood at his cottage gate,
Watching the world go by.
Some people waved and called out a greeting,
Then hurried on by to the friends they were meeting.

The old man's garden was full of weeds
Where once it had been full of flowers.
He remembered the time when he and his wife
Had worked there for long happy hours.

The old man sighed and went back inside;
Sat down in his favourite chair.
He fell asleep in the midday heat
And dreamed that his wife was there.

She smiled at him and held his hand,
'You're old and weary', she said,
'I've waited so long, will you please come?'
The old man nodded his head.

Devotion

I'll leave you to write the end to this poem.

The streets are deserted, the shops are all shut,
A little dog sits on the hospital steps.
His gaze is fixed on the open door;
He dares not move, 'though the wind is raw.
He's been there all night in the wind and the rain
And when night comes, he will be there again.

A patient arrives on a stretcher,
Two men carry it in through the door.
The little dog wags his tail and sniffs;
Then drops his head on his paw.

His throat is dry, no food in his tummy;
Then out through the door comes a child, with his mummy.
He runs down the steps and strokes the dog's head,
He opens his lunch box and takes out some bread,
'You can share my lunch, doggie', he said.

Darkness fell and the dog felt revived,
So, he went to the door and passed on, inside;
He crept down the corridor and sniffed at each door,
Then padded on, each room to explore.

The old man lay still in the hospital bed,
The doctor turned to the nurse, and said,
'He won't last much longer; he's not getting stronger;
He's lost the will to live.'

The dog crouched low in the shadows,
'Til the doctor and nurse left the room,
Then he silently padded across to the bed.
He whined and he woofed, 'It's me', he said.
He licked the man's face; the man stroked the dog's head.
The dog, with pure joy, leaped onto the bed.
They lay there 'til morning,
The search at an end,
The dog and his master, again.
The man and his friend.

Beauty and Heartache

Down in the valley, where the sheep lay sleeping,
And the cows chew their cud in the shallow stream,
Where the squirrels hunt for nuts in the trees'
leafy branches
And the harebells ring in the light summer breeze.

There he lay at the end of life's journey;
His eyes grew dim and his heart grew weak.
He dreamed of the times when he raced
through the meadows,
Gathering in his master's sheep.

A young child lay beside him,
Soothing his journey's end.
So, he wept for the past and he wept for the future;
And he wept for the passing of his loyal, doggy friend.

Alone

I admire the old lady's courage

She lived alone in the family home;
The children had grown up and left.
Her husband passed away last June,
Leaving her feeling bereft.

She'd been so busy; she'd worked so hard;
Everyone needed her, then.
Now she lived alone in the family home;
Would anyone need her again?

She looked round the room, not a thing out of place;
No toys and odd socks littered the place.
She thought of the days when the children were small
And the house was filled with the sound of them all.

She wept, alone, in the family home.
Then, she thought, 'It's all up to me.'
She went to see the young mother, next door,
And invited them all for tea.

After Sunday Worship

Comments I've heard through the years.

Who put those flowers in that alcove?
I've always done that for years.
I'll have a word with the vicar.
I expect it will lead to tears!

Who chose the hymns last Sunday?
I don't like the new ones at all.
Why can't we use a hymn book
And not read the words from the wall?

Why don't they use the organ?
That group can't sing in tune
And as for those guitars,
Well, I nearly left the room.

What's that, Mrs. Grey, what's that you say?
They're going to take out the pews?
Well, that's the last straw, I'll not come anymore.
I'll give the vicar my views!

White Horse Hill

One fine morning, very early, long before the sun was up,
My friends and I climbed White Horse Hill,
Right to the very top.

We lay on our backs on the chalky grass,
Where our ancestors roamed, day and night,
And the rim of the sun climbed over the hill
And flooded the world with light.

While, down in the valley, where the shadows lingered,
Ghostly voices were heard.
We stayed, quite still, on the brow of the hill
And none of us uttered a word!

Memories

*Written after chatting with Tricia and Val
at a church coffee morning,*

Do you remember the days of the mangle,
When the washing was done by hand
And we children turned the handle
And thought that it was grand?

Do you remember the old tin bath
That hung on a nail on the wall?
And do you remember the outside loo
With big black spiders galore?

Do you remember the freezing bedrooms
And the lino on the floor?
Do you remember your fingers and toes
With chilblains, red and raw?

Do you remember the rabbits, hanging outside the butcher's shop,
A pig's head adorning the window with parsley on its top?
Do you remember the milkman delivering milk from a pail,
And a postman, twice a day, bringing round the mail?

I remember the baker, coming round with a horse and cart,
With his lardy cakes and cottage loaves which we loved to pull apart.
We gave the horse an apple, the baker, a cup of tea.
He gave my mum a currant bun and said it was just for me.

If you remember the things I remember,
I've a message just for you –
There's nothing wrong with your memory
Although you're 92!

Val Goodwin

Tricia Clitheroe

Simpler Times

*We didn't have all the toys and gadgets they have today, but
we had our imagination and freedom to roam.*

When I was young, many years ago,
We left our bikes propped up on the kerb.
When we got back, sometime later,
They were still there, quite undisturbed.

We left our babies in prams, outside shops,
While we went inside to explore.
They were always there, when we came back.
They don't do that anymore.

If I was out when the children came home,
The key was left under the mat.
Some folk left their doors unlocked,
But I didn't fancy that.

When school broke up, the children,
Went over the fields to play,
They took lemonade and a sandwich,
And were usually out all day.

Life was much simpler, when I was young.
At least that's how I feel.
Very few cars or telephones,
But there'd always be a hot meal.

Childhood Memories

Not many people could afford coffee pre-war.

'They've got Camp coffee at the corner shop',
My mother said to me, 'Go and buy a bottle for your father,
He likes it better than tea.'

'Hello, Mrs. Coombs, I've come for some Camp coffee.
I can't see where you keep it', I said.
'They're underneath the counter, for the customers I like,
After all, there's a war on, Fred!'

I took the Camp coffee back to my mother.
'Can I have a cup of coffee, please, Mum?'
'No, I'll keep it in the cupboard, especially for your father.
After all, there's a war on, son.'

Mummy called from the kitchen, 'The butcher had some suet,
So, I'm making a steamed pudding; come and help me do it.
Cut that rasher of bacon, cut it up nice and small.
Then, put it in the mixture, so there is some for us all.'

Mum gave me a farthing. I took it to the shop.
'Hello, Mrs. Lewis, have you got a lollipop?'
'Have you brought your ration book?
No points, no sweets,' she said.
'Come back another day.
You know there's a war on, Fred.'

Mum has a treadle sewing machine,
Which she treadles far into the night.
She's made me a coat from an army blanket;
I hope I will look alright.'

She's making blouses of finest silk,
Which came from a parachute panel.
The pilot baled out, before the plane crashed,
And he came down in the channel.'

We carried our gas masks wherever we went,
To keep us safe and sound.
Now, seventy years later we're all wearing face masks;
And so, the world goes round!

Today and Yester Year

I decided to have an outside tap so that
I could water my flowers.
The plumber agreed to come on Saturday,
Outside his usual hours.

I cleared out the cupboard under the sink
And thought I could open a shop!
There were cleaning products of every kind,
And even two bottles of pop.

There was a bottle of fluid to remove sticky labels,
And one to remove spots from the carpet.
A bar of something to hang in the loo
To mask the smell of the Harpic.

Washing up liquid of every kind,
Hand wash, hand gel – what a find!
A mystery packet marked 1 and 9
And something to squirt to keep the air fine.

When we were married, seventy years ago,

This cupboard held nothing like these,

Just Lifebuoy soap and a scrubbing brush,

Soda and elbow grease!

Please Mum

We've all been there!

Tell me a story, Mummy, a story of long ago,
When a handsome prince on a snow-white horse
Searched for a girl to marry, of course.
Tell me a story, do!

Why did Doctor Foster go to Gloucester in the rain?
Why did he fall in a puddle, Mummy?
Why didn't he go there again?

Why did Cinderella wear her slippers to the ball?
Why did the old woman swallow a fly?
I don't understand it at all.

Why did Jack and Jill go up the hill for water?
Why didn't they turn the tap on, Mummy?
Why did Jack wear a crown?
Did they see the Duke of York, marching his men up and down?

Who ate the three bears porridge, Mummy?
Why did she break baby's chair?

Why did she sleep in his bed, Mummy?
I feel sorry for that baby bear.

Why was King Cole such a merry old soul?
Did he see Humpty Dumpty fall?
Why couldn't the king's men put him together again
And put him back on the wall?

When the wolf ate Granny, did it eat her clothes as well?
Why did the pigs build a house of straw?
And what's that awful smell?

Tell me a story, Mummy, a story of long ago.
Why did the princess lie on a pea?
I really want to know.

How many wives had Henry the Eighth?
Why was Henry so Bad?
Tell me a story, Mummy.
NO! GO ASK YOUR DAD!

Why?

Things people tell me!

Why can't I read a paper or book?

Why are my eyes growing dim?

Tell me, what is wrong with my voice?

I used to love to sing.

Why can't I walk up hills anymore?

And why can't I ride my bike?

Why does my chest rumble and wheeze?

Oh, why can't I do as I like?

I don't know the answer to all these questions,

But I know this, without any doubt:

I've outlived my cooker and freezer

And their guarantee has run out!

Good Morning, Bill

There's old Bill, coming down the path;

We'll have a nice long chat.

He's lost his hair and put on weight,

But I'll not tell him that.

I see he's got another dog.

The last one bit his wife.

She survived, but the dog dropped dead.

It was shock, the coroner said.

But I'll not tell him that!

Poor old Bill, he needs a shave.

He's let himself go. He's showing his age.

He'd look much smarter in a hat,

But I'll not tell him that.

'Morning, Bill', I call to him, 'You're looking very fit.

We all slow down at 92 and need a walking stick.

Let's stand here and have a nice chat.

We'll talk about the weather'.

'I'm only 75', he says, 'and I'm not Bill, I'm Trevor!'

Trevor

I can see Trevor, coming down the High Street;
We can have a nice long chat.
He's coming very slowly, and he's walking with a limp.
I'll take him in this café for a cookie and a drink.

'Good morning, Trevor', I call to him. He looks the other way.
So, I tap him on the arm, and say to him,
'Come into this café for a cookie and a coffee,
My treat, I'll pay!'

When we find a table, where we can sit together,
I take a closer look at him, 'What's the matter, Trevor?
You're looking very pale. Are you underneath the weather?
I hope that you're not sickening for the 'flu!'

'There's nothing wrong with me, the problem is with you.
Please go and pay the money at the till.
I'm not one to complain, but if we meet again,
Please don't call me Trevor, I am Bill!'

71

Bill and Trevor

Based on a true story

'Good morning, Trevor, Good morning, Bill!
How are you today?
I haven't seen you for ages.
Have you been away?'

'Are you feeling ill, Bill?'
'No, it is my wife;
She's gone off dogs forever, Trevor,
Since she nearly lost her life!'

'What happened to the dog, Bill,
Since it took that bite?'
'I gave it to my brother, Phil,
Who kept it overnight.

Then, it bit the postman.
So, it had to be put down;
They took it to the local vet,
Who charged them half a crown!'

'My brother, Phil, sent me the bill
And said I had to pay.
Then, the door burst open;
The dog had run away.

It yapped at me, in pure delight;
My wife leapt from her bed.
I decided I would keep the dog
And send my wife away instead!'

Holy Howlers – all true!
Humour is mankind's greatest blessing - Mark Twain

The ladies of the church have cast off clothing of every kind, and they can be seen in the church basement Friday afternoon.

For those of you who have children and don't know it, we have a nursery downstairs.

This Easter Sunday, we will ask Mrs White to come forward and lay an egg on the altar.

Thursday at 5pm, there will be a meeting of the Little Mothers Club. All wishing to become little mothers will please meet with the minister in the study.

The choir will meet at the Larsen house for fun and sinning.

Remember in prayer the many who are sick of our church and community.

Next Sunday Mrs Vinson will be soloist for the morning service. The pastor will then speak on 'It's a Terrible Experience.'

Potluck supper: prayer and medication to follow.

Don't let worry kill you off – let the church help.

On Sunday a special collection will be taken to defray the expense of the new carpet. All those wishing to do something on the carpet will please come forward to get a piece of paper.

Have you ever seen an Angel?
This was a true event.

The cruise ship docked on a foreign shore.
We disembarked and set off to explore.
We went, by bus, to the centre of town;
Admired the buildings where we were set down.

We walked down a quaint alley with cute little shops,
Selling pastries and sweetmeats, T-shirts and frocks.
We entered a church, with gold statues and carving;
Outside, in the porch, the beggars were starving.

'It's time to get back', we said to each other.
But which way to go, we'd yet to discover!
No one we asked understood what we said,
So, we walked with our backs to the sun, instead.

We hurried along for an hour and a half, and then we smelled the sea.
Delighted, we came to the end of the path, but gazed despairingly,
Twin railway lines ran from right to left,
Between ourselves and the sea.
No sign of a bridge or a tunnel and no one to tell us the way.
What do we do when life's pathway gets rough? We close our eyes and pray.

When we opened our eyes, a young man stood before us.
He addressed us in English.
'Please help us,' we chorused, 'we need to cross over
the line'.

'No problem', he said, 'Do you see there, ahead,
Where the bushes grow over the path?
Behind there's a tunnel going under the line;
Sometimes it's flooded, but today it is fine'.

'It's muddy and dark, but please, don't take fright,
Keep looking ahead and you'll soon see the light'.
We must thank that young man for seeing our plight.
We turned round to shake hands,
BUT
He vanished from sight.

Nobody

He sat, alone, in the doorway
On a freezing, winter street.
Nobody gave him a second glance
And nobody noticed his feet.

She lay in the gutter, starving,
In a far-off land.
Nobody gave her a second look
And nobody noticed her hand.

A child shuffled past, on his bottom,
On the eve of Eastertide.
And nobody noticed his wasted legs
And nobody saw his side.

The world hurried by, on Good Friday.
'It's a holiday', someone cried.
And nobody noticed the wounded man,
Or saw His hands, feet and side.

Destination

When I started this poem, I'd no idea how it would end. It just wrote itself.

The infant stream wanders through meadows and pastures,
Dappled by the sun, as it ripples on its way.
Mothers bring their children, eager and bare footed,
To splash among the shallows, as they play.

'Where are you going, O infant stream?'
'What is your vision, what is your dream?'
'I dream of the past, the present is mine,
I leave the future to The One who's divine.'

'I'm tired', said the stream, 'I'll flow under that bridge
And rest, in the shade, to recover.'
While he is there, he hears a voice call,
'Come and join me, my brother'.

The tired little stream crept out of the shadows,
'I can't flow much further', he cried.
Then, a mighty river scooped him up in his arms
And carried him away with the tide.

The bullrushes stood to attention,
The willows bowed their heads.
The harebells rang with jubilation,
As river and stream rushed ahead.

The cows came down, with soulful eyes,
To watch with fascination,
As river and stream rushed with gathering speed
Towards its destination.

Swans with their cygnets and ducks with their brood,
Paddle against the tide.
People in towns hung over the bridge
To watch the river glide.

Countryside, villages, cities and fields,
What can the hurry be?
Then, it reaches the top of a towering cliff
And hurtles down to the sea.

Mrs. Brown

There's a pigeon in my garden; I don't like pigeons at all.

I wish he'd not do his courting in the sight of us all.

There's a strange dog in my garden; I don't like dogs at all.

He's eating the crumbs I put out for the birds, no,

I don't like dogs at all.

There's the postman in my garden; I don't like him at all.

He brings me bills and if I'm not in, he posts them

through the door.

There are children in my garden, looking for their ball.

I like to see children playing; I don't mind them at all.

There's the milkman in my garden; I don't mind him at all.

He brings me potatoes, milk and eggs.

He knows I have trouble with my legs,

So, I don't mind him at all.

My garden is quite busy, I think you will agree.

But there's one thing missing, as I look from my kitchen;

I have no flowers, you see.

I'd like a cottage garden, where I can sit out for hours.

Then, I could invite those I don't like

To sit with me and my flowers.

That Naughty Imp

There's an imp, who lives in my wardrobe;

He hides what I want to wear.

I search, in vain, for my blouse and skirt;

I know that it is there.

I need to go out shopping.

I don't really want to do it,

But when I go for the keys of the car,

That imp has beaten me to it!

My friend is coming to dinner.

Where is the tablecloth?

I put it away the other day;

That imp must have whisked it off.

I'd make myself a cup of tea,

But the lid on the milk is screwed tight.

I know that little imp is to blame.

I heard him about in the night.

I made myself some buttered toast,

Spread thick with marmalade.

But before I could take a single bite,

It was knocked from my hand, face down, I'm afraid.

There's a sound outside my window

And there I see, on the path,

That naughty imp, who calls, with a wink,

'I'll be back, in an hour and a half!!'

I wish

I have written 100 poems during Lockdown,

enough for two more books.

I wish I wasn't so short,

I wish I wasn't so fat.

I've always wished I was tall

And that my tummy was flat.

I wish that boy, I fancy,

Would send me a Valentine card,

And I wish that he would kiss me,

Behind the shed in the yard.

I wish that he would tell me

He loves me, lots and lots;

I wish that I didn't blush when I see him

And I wish that I didn't have spots.

I wish I was good at gymnastics,
I wish I was good at maths.
I wish we didn't have sprouts for dinner
And I don't like corned beef hash.

I wish my hair wasn't curly,
I wish my hair wasn't black.
I wish that man wouldn't call me 'girly'
And give me a slap on my back!

I wish it wasn't raining,
I wish the sun would shine,
Then, I could go on a bike ride -
I'll be back by supper time.

If you, my friends, feel sorry for me,
Don't give me a second look.
The only thing I wish for is ...
That I could finish this book!

The Bright Side

Diana Merriman told me that they were held up in a traffic jam for 55 minutes. She certainly saw the bright side.

If you always look on the bright side,
The bright side will shine upon you.
They were travelling along the A27,
When a traffic jam came into view.

Where is the bright side in that? you may ask.
They could be there for hours.
They came to a stop by a high grassy bank,
Dotted with hundreds of pretty wild flowers.

Pink, yellow, blue and white; nature's offering for their delight;
Dog daisies, knapweed, everlasting sweet peas,
Ragwort, scabious and vetch.
But the jewel in the crown, on the high grassy brink,
Shone orchids of deepest pink.

I Don't Understand

I don't understand why two thirds of the world is starving.

I don't understand why some countries are always at war.

I don't understand why small children get cancer

And why some folk break the law.

I don't understand why so many people say

they believe in God

And yet they don't believe in the church;

I think that's rather odd.

I don't understand why those with strong views,

impose them on another.

Why can't they agree to differ and show respect

for each other.

I don't understand all the Bible;

All of its ancient laws.

But I can't pick and choose the parts that I like

And those I don't like, ignore.

But this I do understand, we are all made in the

image of God;

And if God is love, we must love one another,

And stretch out our hands to each sister and brother,

All prejudices putting aside,

And cherish and nourish the church, God's bride.

The Prodigal Son

Luke 15:11-31

He hated life on his father's farm;

The hard work, as each day unfurled.

He asked his father for his inheritance

And set out to explore the world.

He made his way to the city streets;

Lived a life of wine, women and song.

He had lots of friends, until, one day,

They found all his money had gone!

Nobody helped him, nobody cared;

For this life, he lived, he was quite unprepared.

His clothes were in rags, no shoes on his feet;

Nowhere to live and nothing to eat.

He trudged around the countryside;

Looking for work and a bed.

He espied a man in a farmyard,

'You can feed my pigs', he said.

He spent his days in the pigsty,

Sharing their bed and their swill.

'If I go on like this', he said to himself,

'I'll become mortally ill'.

'My father is a good man;

He treats his servants as friends.

I'll go back home and plead with him

To let me work with them'.

His father never gave up hope.

His heart within him did yearn.

He spent many hours, scanning the road,

Willing his boy to return.

The old man sat in the doorway;

His eyes were growing dim.

Then, he saw in the distance, a figure,

Drawing closer to him.

The father sprang to his feet

And hurried as fast as he could.

With arms open wide, he gathered his son

And the years slipped away as together they clung.

The servants stood at a distance.

'This day, my life is complete.

Bring a fine robe, a ring for his finger

And sandals for his bruised feet'.

'Go, kill the fatted calf and organize a feast;

Call in all our neighbours and friends.

My son was dead, but now he lives!

Was lost, yet now he's found.

And this place where we stand

Is hallowed ground'.

Seeking the Lost

Inspired by a parable Jesus told.

Luke 15: 1-7

High on the hill tops, where the air was pure and bright,

A shepherd boy played his pipe.

He loved all the flock and knew each by sight,

As he carefully guarded them, both day and night.

When the time came for the sheep to be sheared,

He gathered them all around.

With woolly heads, bleating and nudging and shoving,

They followed him down to the ground.

They were healthy and strong and their fleeces were thick;

He looked at his flock with pride.

Then, his loving eyes saw that something was wrong;

There were just 99 by his side!

One of his precious sheep was missing

On the hilltops, far away,

Where the wild beasts prowled in the darkness,

Seeking a lonely stray.

He left the 99 behind,

In the safety of the fold.

He climbed the rocky slopes again,

As darkness fell, and the air grew cold.

He climbed the old, familiar tracks,

He searched the grassy mounds.

He felt his way over jutting crags,

But not a trace of the sheep as found.

The shepherd boy called the creature, by name,

He heard a plaintive bleat.

A shaft of moonlight pierced the clouds

And lighted a path to the sheep.

It lay twisted and torn in a cruel web of thorns.

It had tried to go on its way.

The rest of the flock had followed their master;

It was safer to trust and obey.

How gently the shepherd released the sheep,

How lovingly spoke its name.

He lifted it on his shoulder

And carried it home again.

The Good Samaritan

Luke 10:25-37

He was travelling, alone, on the stony road,

Jericho lay ahead,

When a band of robbers, leapt from cover.

They stripped him and beat him

And left him half dead!

A travelling priest, on his way to the temple,

Saw the man where he lay.

Not wishing to make himself unclean,

He continued on his way.

A Levite, bound for the city, heard a feeble cry,

But he had to attend to religious duties.

So, he left him there

And hurried on by.

The poor man's body was wracked with pain.

He struggled for every breath,

And as the day grew shorter,

The man was approaching death.

A Samaritan, as he journeyed, came where the victim lay.

He tended his wounds with oil and wine,

Binding him up with linen, fine

And placed him on his donkey.

The donkey, carefully, trotted along

Conscious of his precious load;

The Samaritan knew of an inn, ahead,

Further on down the road.

He carried the man up to his room,

And tended him night and day.

The time drew nigh, when he said to his friend,

'Now you are stronger, I'll tarry no longer,

I must be on my way.'

He gave the inn keeper two silver coins;

'Take care of him', he said.

'And when I come again, this way,

If you've spent more, I will repay.'

Jesus told this parable to the expert in the law.

Then he looked at him and said,

'Who do you think was neighbour to the man

who was nearly dead?

'The one who showed mercy', the expert replied.

Jesus looked on him with love in his eyes,

'Then you go and do likewise', he said.

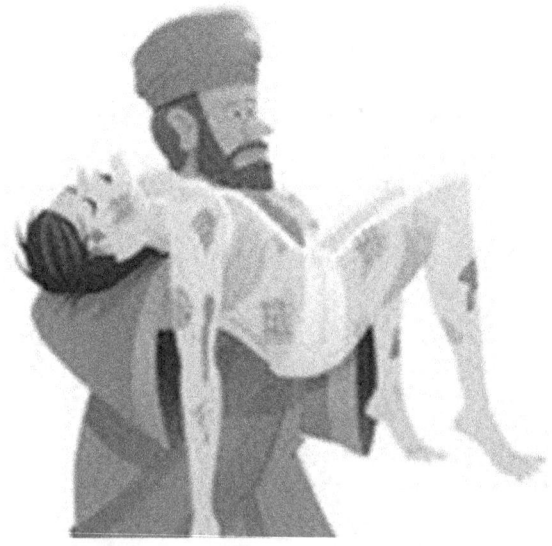

Hand in Hand

They walked down the pathway of life together;

They walked down it, hand in hand.

They laughed and they cried as they met joy and sorrow

And sought God's protection for each day and morrow.

They lived their lives making memories,

For each generation to find.

When children were born and took their first steps,

They prayed that their pathway was kind.

When their children were grown, the old folk were alone.

They were both loving and kind.

Still, hand in hand, they walked on life's pathway.

A very long road lay behind.

The pathway led to a narrow door; only room for one to

pass through.

'I'll go in first', the weary man said.

'I'll be waiting inside for you'.

As the old woman wept, her Saviour stood there,

Waiting to help her through.

A Rough Patch

When the pathway through life becomes stony and steep,

And sometimes you stumble and fall,

Get back on your feet, brush yourself down,

Pull back your shoulders, walk tall!

Lift your eyes to the top of the hill,

Let the healing tears flow, as they certainly will.

When you reach the top, there's a wonderful view,

As the sun breaks through and soaks up the dew.

Beyond, life's pathway lies smooth and wide

And invites you to walk on its sunny side.

So, wrap up your memories, hold them close to your heart

And walk together along life's path.

Life's Pathway

Based on the 23rd Psalm

Thank you, my friend for your company,
As we've trodden the Pathway of Life.
We've wept in the shadows and danced in the meadows,
Where the wild flower grows and the quiet stream flows
And swallows swoop high in the heavens.

When the path grew rough and narrow,
And the way ahead, unclear,
I dreamed of the flowers in the meadow and felt no fear
As we dwelt in the valley of shadows,
For you were always near.

Singing melted the darkness,
The way ahead was bright.
Then, hand in hand, we stepped from life's pathway
Into the glorious light.

www.ingramcontent.com/pod-product-compliance
Lightning Source LLC
LaVergne TN
LVHW011729060526
838200LV00051B/3090